CCSS **Genre** Folktale

W9-AWQ-728

Essential Question
What is a folktale?

The
Storytelling
Stone

retold by Amy Helfer
illustrated by Diane Paterson

Chapter 1

Grandfather Stone

Once upon a time, a boy lived at the edge of a village. His name was Crow.

Crow had no one to take care of him. His clothes were shabby, and his face was dirty.

Crow didn't have any time for playing. He was busy taking care of himself.

He had to clean his hut. He had to get his own food, and he had to cook it.

Crow hunted in the woods every day. He traded his catch for corn and beans.

One day, Crow sat down to rest. He leaned against a large stone. He was nearly asleep when he heard a voice.

"May I tell you a story?" the voice asked.

Crow jumped up and looked around. He didn't see anyone. "Who's there?" he asked. "Show yourself!"

"It is me, Grandfather Stone," said the voice. Crow noticed a face take shape in the large stone.

"I won't hurt you," said the stone. "I just want to tell you a story."

Chapter 2

Crow Hears the Stories

"What is a story?" Crow asked.

Grandfather Stone told him. "Stories tell about everything that happened before now."

Crow sat down. Grandfather Stone began to tell Crow about a time long before this one.

First, he told him a story about how birds got wings. Next, he told how fish learned to swim.

Hours later, Grandfather Stone was tired. "Go home," he told Crow. "Come back tomorrow, and I will tell you more."

Crow went back to his village. He traded his birds for a hot supper. Then he went to sleep.

Day after day, Crow listened to
stories. Finally, Grandfather Stone
said, "That is all I know. Now you
know it, too. Pass on all my stories,
so they will never be forgotten."

Chapter 3
Crow Tells the Stories

Crow went back home and packed up his things. The next day, he left his village. After walking many miles, Crow reached another village. He told the people all the stories.

The people were happy to hear the stories. They gave Crow many gifts.

Crow walked from village to village, telling his stories. After many years, he returned home. Now he was a grown man. The people didn't know who he was!

They invited Crow to sit by the fire, and they shared their food. Afterwards, Crow began to tell his stories.

When he was finished, Crow said, "Tell these stories to your children and grandchildren. Now that you know the stories of our people, you must never forget them."

This is how stories began. This is why there are storytellers today. Whenever you hear stories about your people, listen—and pass them on.

Respond to Reading

Retell

Use your own words to retell *The Storytelling Stone.*

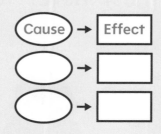

Text Evidence

1. Look at pages 2 and 3. Why didn't Crow have time to play? Cause and Effect

2. Look at page 10. Why didn't the people know who Crow was? Cause and Effect

3. How do you know that *The Storytelling Stone* is a folktale? Genre

Compare Texts
Read a song about family stories.

Family Stories

by Amy Helfer

When Dad was the same age as me,
He used to sit on Grandpa's knee.
Grandpa told what he enjoyed
When he was just a little boy.

Stories about the games he played,
The names of all the friends he made,
The places that he walked to,
And the people that he talked to.

Now I sit near my father's knee,
And he tells those tales to me.
He tells me his own stories, too,
About the things he used to do.

One day when I am fully grown,
I may have children of my own.
And like my father used to do
I'll tell them all my stories, too.

Make Connections

Look at both selections. Why are stories important? What can stories teach us? Text to Text

Focus on Genre

Folktale A folktale is a story based on traditions and customs. Folktales have been passed along through the years by telling them aloud. Folktales often teach lessons.

What to Look for In *The Storytelling Stone,* a stone tells Crow how everything happened before now. In real life, stones do not speak.

Your Turn

Write a folktale that explains why something in nature is the way it is. Draw a picture to go with your story. Share your folktale and drawing with the class.